T0389986

NATIVE
AMERICAN
NATIONS

THE SHOSHONE

BY BETTY MARCKS

CONSULTANT: TIM TOPPER,
CHEYENNE RIVER SIOUX

BLASTOFF!
DISCOVERY

BELLWETHER MEDIA • MINNEAPOLIS, MN

Blastoff! Discovery launches a new mission: reading to learn. Filled with facts and features, each book offers you an exciting new world to explore!

BLASTOFF! UNIVERSE

BLASTOFF! Beginners — GRADE K

BLASTOFF! READERS — GRADES 1-3

BLASTOFF! DISCOVERY — GRADE 4

This edition first published in 2026 by Bellwether Media, Inc.

Library of Congress Cataloging-in-Publication Data

LC record for The Shoshone available at: https://lccn.loc.gov/2025018375

Editor: Elizabeth Neuenfeldt   Series Designer: Andrea Schneider
Book Designer: Laura Sowers

Printed in the United States of America, North Mankato, MN.

TABLE OF CONTENTS

The Shoshone are **descendants** of Native Americans who called themselves *Newe*. This means "The People." There are three main Shoshone groups. They are the Eastern Shoshone, the Northern Shoshone, and the Western Shoshone.

Shoshone people have lived in the **Great Basin** region for thousands of years. Their homelands cover areas of what is now California, Idaho, Nevada, Utah, and Wyoming. The Wind River Mountain range in Wyoming is home to the Eastern Shoshone. The Northern Shoshone mostly live in Idaho. The Western Shoshone are mostly in Nevada.

IDAHO

WYOMING

NEVADA

UTAH

CALIFORNIA

N W E S

■ EASTERN SHOSHONE
■ NORTHERN SHOSHONE
■ WESTERN SHOSHONE

WIND RIVER
MOUNTAIN RANGE
IN WYOMING

TRADITIONAL SHOSHONE LIFE

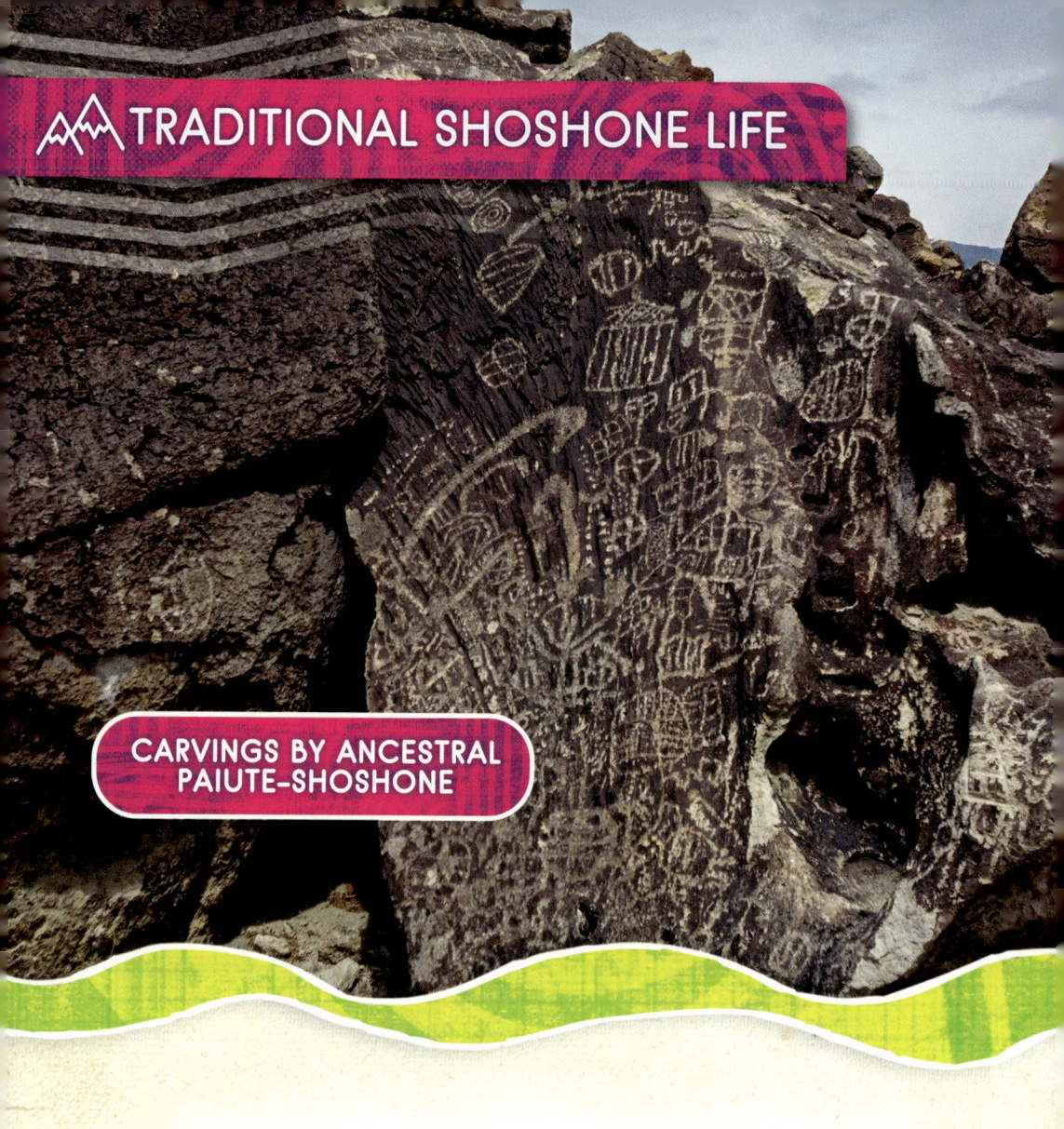

CARVINGS BY ANCESTRAL PAIUTE-SHOSHONE

Ancestral Shoshone had a deep understanding and connection to the earth. This allowed them to live well in the harsh Great Basin. They believed all things that came from Earth were **sacred**. They believed all plants, animals, and the land had a spirit. The Shoshone respected all natural things. They only used what they needed. These beliefs are still practiced by many Shoshone today.

Most ancestral Shoshone lived in small family groups for most of the year. These groups often included extended family members. Smaller groups came together each winter to camp.

A SACRED SHOSHONE SITE CALLED BEAR LODGE OR DEVILS TOWER

Ancestral Shoshone were **seminomadic**. They traveled with the seasons to hunt and gather food. They collected seeds and berries in spring and summer. They also gathered vegetables such as wild potatoes and garlic. They collected nuts in fall.

Ancestral Shoshone hunted small animals such as rabbits in summer. They hunted large animals like deer, sheep, and bison in fall. Salmon was an important food for some groups. Many Shoshone also ate ducks, geese, grasshoppers, and crickets.

SOURCE OF PINE NUTS

HORSES

Horses eventually became an important part of the culture for some Shoshone bands. The Wind River Shoshone and Northern Shoshone may have had horses as early as 1680.

TIPIS

The type of shelter ancestral Shoshone used depended on the seasons. For some groups, summer homes included leafy branches laid over pole frames. Groups left these shelters behind as they moved. People may have also used caves as places to rest.

Some ancestral Shoshone used tipis throughout the year. These shelters provided warmth and protection during winter. They were cool in summer. These homes included large pole frames covered in large animal hides. The hides were often decorated. Scenes from dreams or acts of bravery were common. People also drew animals and other designs on hides.

SHOSHONE RESOURCES

TIPI

AROUND 10 TO 12 BISON HIDES

AROUND 20 TO 25 PINE POLES

ILLUSTRATION OF SACAGAWEA WITH LEWIS AND CLARK

One of the first recorded contacts that ancestral Shoshone had with white people was in 1805. The Akaitikka, or Lemhi Shoshone, met members of the Lewis and Clark **Expedition**. The Akaitikka provided horses and supplies to the group. A Lemhi Shoshone woman named Sacagawea was part of the expedition. She was reunited with her family during this meeting.

Other Shoshone groups began to encounter fur traders and **settlers** during the first half of the 1800s. Westward expansion and the discovery of gold and silver brought more people to Shoshone lands. These newcomers treated the land as their own and misused resources.

SACAGAWEA

Sacagawea was around 17 years old when she began traveling with Lewis and Clark. Sacagawea's skills and knowledge helped keep men in the group alive.

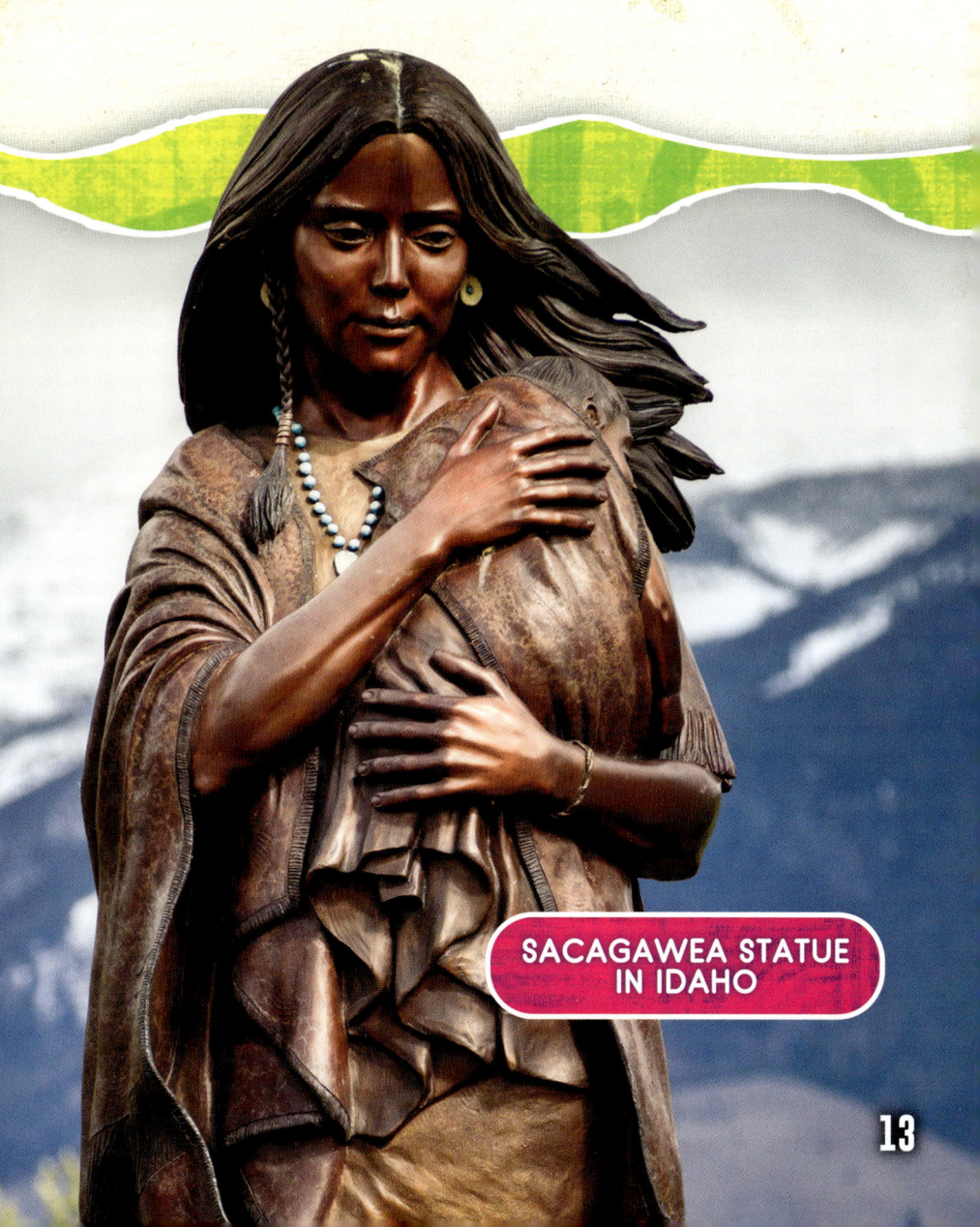

SACAGAWEA STATUE IN IDAHO

Tensions grew in the mid-1800s. Some Shoshone groups began to defend their lands and **cultures**. They targeted wagon trains and other groups of white people. The U.S. government soon stepped in. The U.S. Army attacked a group of Shoshone on the Bear River in January 1863. This attack is called the Bear River Massacre. It was one of the worst attacks on Native American peoples in history.

The U.S. government forced Shoshone **bands** to sign **treaties** and live on **reservations**. The U.S. often broke these treaties. They took more Shoshone lands. But the Shoshone did not give up. They kept fighting for their rights.

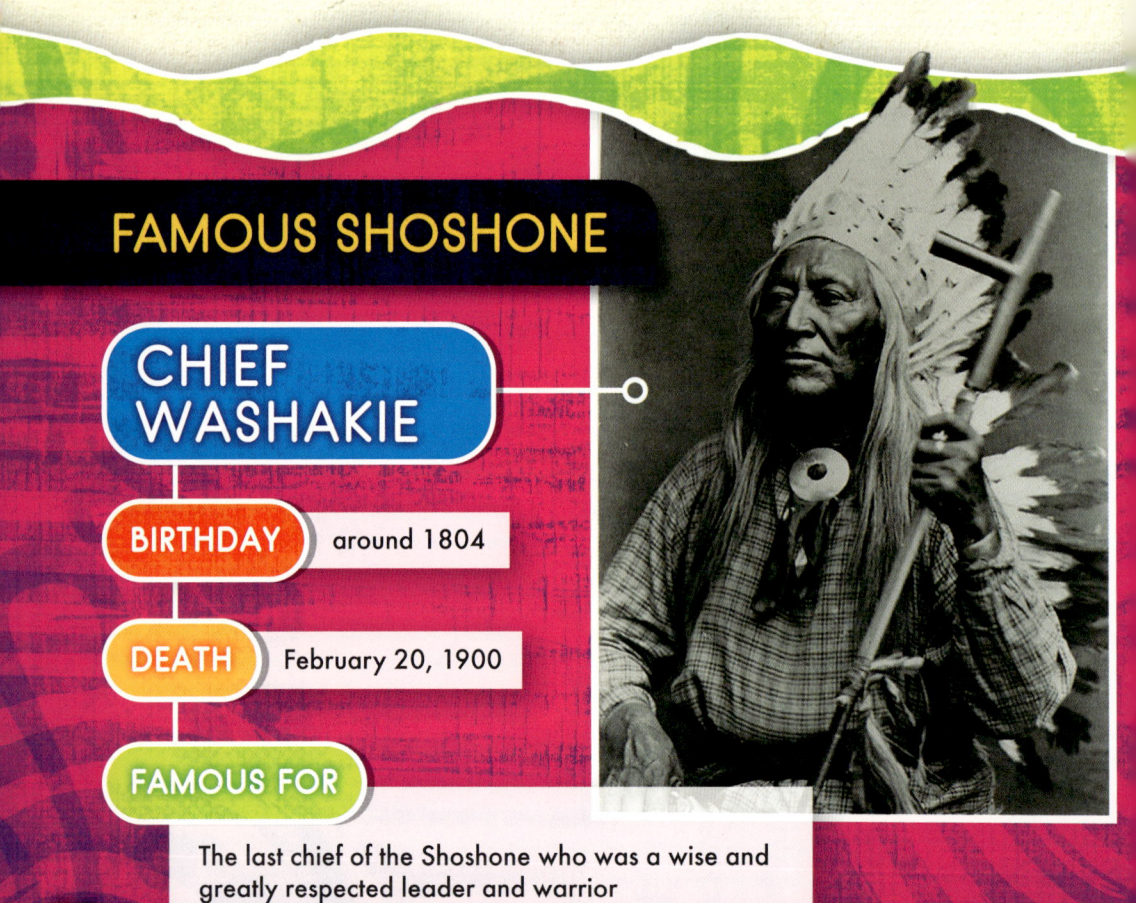

FAMOUS SHOSHONE

CHIEF WASHAKIE

BIRTHDAY around 1804

DEATH February 20, 1900

FAMOUS FOR

The last chief of the Shoshone who was a wise and greatly respected leader and warrior

SITE OF THE BEAR
RIVER MASSACRE

FORCED CHANGE

Many Shoshone children were forced to go to boarding
schools starting in the late 1800s. They were forced to
give up their traditions and way of life at the schools.
They were forced to learn white culture.

Today, the Shoshone nation consists of many tribes. Some of the tribes have formed communities with other nations, such as the Paiute. There are currently 12 Shoshone tribes federally recognized by the U.S. Other tribes are recognized by state governments. Their reservations and lands are in California, Idaho, Nevada, Oregon, Utah, and Wyoming.

Many tribal members live and work on the reservations. But Shoshone also live throughout the U.S. and the world. Some members work as farmers or ranchers. Others work for tribal businesses or in **tourism**. Shoshone also work in health care, education, technology, and many other fields.

WYOMING

N
W—E
S

■ WIND RIVER RESERVATION

Shoshone tribes and bands are independent nations. Their governments are run by tribal **councils** or business councils. Council members are elected. They work for their tribal members. They oversee tribal land uses, make budgets, and make important decisions for their tribes.

GOVERNMENT OF THE SHOSHONE-BANNOCK TRIBES OF THE FORT HALL RESERVATION

Fort Bridger Treaty of 1868

EXECUTIVE OFFICE

7-MEMBER FORT HALL BUSINESS COUNCIL

TRIBAL COURTS

SHOSHONE-BANNOCK
CASINO HOTEL

Each tribal government provides services to its members. These services create stronger communities. Many have police forces that enforce laws. Governments also provide health and education services. Many tribes own businesses that earn money to run these services. They own casinos, hotels, museums, and more.

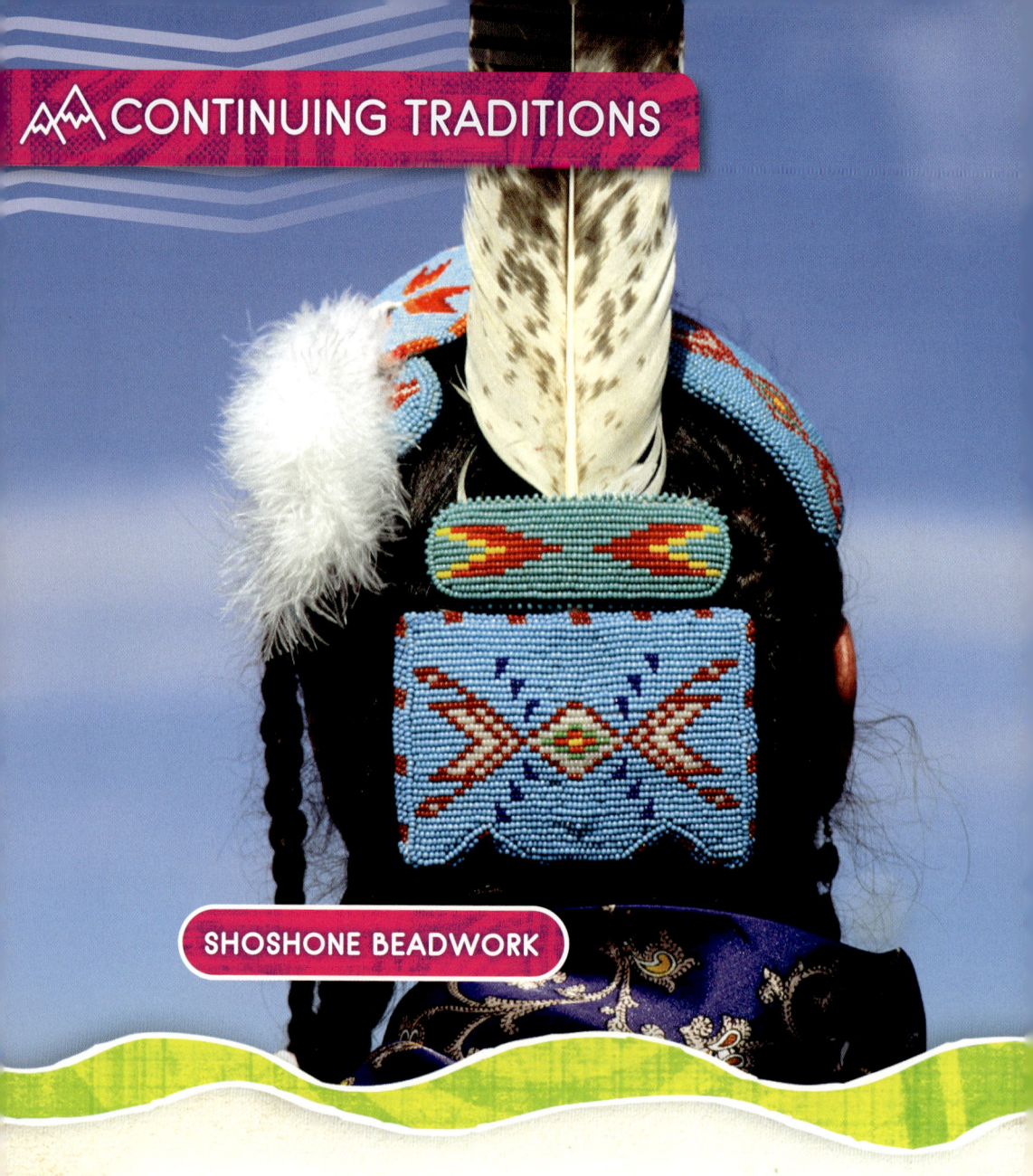

SHOSHONE BEADWORK

Many Shoshone practice the **traditions** of their ancestors. Ancestral Shoshone used woven baskets to collect and prepare food and medicine. Skilled weavers teach those who want to carry on the traditions of their ancestors. The Great Basin Native Basket Weavers Association offers classes to members. Its goal is to keep basket weaving alive for another thousand years.

Beadwork is another tradition practiced by some Shoshone artists. They use colorful beads and traditional materials. These include buckskin to create clothing, bags, moccasins, and other items.

WESTERN SHOSHONE BASKET WEAVING

WILLOW

SUMAC

WESTERN SHOSHONE BASKET

Another way some Shoshone practice their culture and traditions is by practicing their language. The Shoshone-Bannock Tribes' language program teaches language classes. It also teaches members tribal history. The Eastern Shoshone tribe released a language **app** in 2024. It is called Newe Daygwap. It is a major step in helping people learn the language of their ancestors.

NEWE DAYGWAP LANGUAGE APP

EASTERN SHOSHONE INDIAN DAYS POW WOW

Many Shoshone celebrate their culture and traditions at **Pow Wows**. The Eastern Shoshone host many Pow Wows each summer. Dance is one of the most important elements of the Pow Wows. Each dance includes special drumming and singing. Dancers often wear important clothing.

Mines have harmed Shoshone lands and sacred sites for decades. Tribes have taken mining companies to court to stop them from damaging the land.

Tribes have had some success. The Shoshone-Bannock Tribes won a case in 2021. It proved a mining company's waste was dangerous to nearby lands, people, and animals. The mining company was forced to clean up the waste. Tribes have also faced challenges. A judge ruled against tribes trying to stop mining in 2023. Mining would destroy the site of an 1865 massacre. But the Shoshone will not give up.

SACRED WATER VALLEY

Great Basin tribes are working to get a sacred massacre site named a national monument. It would be called *Bahsahwahbee* National Monument. *Bahsahwahbee* is a Shoshone word. It means "Sacred Water Valley."

Shoshone tribes lead many programs to protect their culture. The Bear River is an important site for many Shoshone. The Northwestern Band of the Shoshone Nation is restoring the land. They plant native plants and remove **invasive species**. They are also restoring the area's wetlands.

SHOSHONE-PAIUTE GREENHOUSE

A GROWING HERD

The Eastern Shoshone Buffalo Program began in 2016 with 10 buffalo. There were 99 buffalo in early 2024!

The Eastern Shoshone have a successful buffalo program. It brings back herds that were absent from the area for over 100 years. The program is one of the many ways Shoshone culture lives on!

LATE 1600s

Some Shoshone bands acquire horses and gradually move toward a Plains culture

1840s

White settlers begin traveling through Shoshone lands

1867

The Fort Hall Reservation is established

1805

The Lemhi Shoshone meet the Lewis and Clark Expedition

1863

The Bear River Massacre occurs

EARLY 1900s

Lemhi Shoshone are forcibly moved from their homelands to the Fort Hall Reservation in what is called the "Lemhi Trail of Tears"

2024

The Eastern Shoshone Tribe releases a Shoshone language app

1868

The Treaty of Fort Bridger is signed, creating the boundaries of the Wind River Reservation

2018

The Northwestern Band of the Shoshone Nation buys ancestral land at the Bear River Massacre site

1983

The Timbisha Shoshone Tribe is federally recognized

GLOSSARY

ancestral—related to relatives who lived long ago

app—a program such as a game or internet browser; an app is also called an application.

bands—groups of people who live as communities and share a culture

councils—groups of people who meet to run governments

cultures—the beliefs, arts, and ways of life in places or societies

descendants—people related to a person or group of people who lived at an earlier time

expedition—a journey taken for a specific reason, such as to explore a region

Great Basin—a region of the U.S. that includes most of Nevada and parts of California, Idaho, Oregon, Utah, and Wyoming

invasive species—plants or animals that are not originally from the area; invasive species often cause harm to their new environments.

Pow Wows—Native American gatherings that usually include dancing

reservations—lands set aside by the U.S. government for the forced removal of Native American communities from their original lands

sacred—relating to spiritual or religious practice

seminomadic—relating to people who move with the seasons

settlers—people who move to live in a new region

tourism—the business of people traveling to visit other places

traditions—customs, ideas, and beliefs handed down from one generation to the next

treaties—official agreements between two groups

TO LEARN MORE

AT THE LIBRARY

Kirkman, Marissa. *Bison*. Mendota Heights, Minn.: Apex Editions, 2025.

Marcks, Betty. *The Sioux*. Minneapolis, Minn.: Bellwether Media, 2024.

Orr, Nicole K. *Sacagawea*. Kennett Square, Penn.: Purple Toad Publishing, 2019.

ON THE WEB

FACTSURFER

Factsurfer.com gives you a safe, fun way to find more information.

1. Go to www.factsurfer.com.

2. Enter "the Shoshone" into the search box and click 🔍.

3. Select your book cover to see a list of related content.

INDEX